INNOVATIVE METHODS
of using AI

for Precise Irrigation of Individual Crops

Author:
Maxwell Steinbeck

PUBLISHING PLATFORM: AMAZON KINDLE DIRECT PUBLISHING
2024

Content

1. **Introduction**
   - Why precision irrigation is the future of agriculture
   - Strategic importance of water resources
   - Using artificial intelligence to optimize irrigation
2. **Basics of precision irrigation**
   - What is precision irrigation?
   - Technological advantages and challenges of traditional irrigation
   - Innovative approaches to water resources management
3. **The role of artificial intelligence in irrigation systems**
   - Use of sensors and sensors to monitor soil moisture
   - Prediction and automation of watering based on AI data
   - Examples of AI application in agriculture
4. **Integrating AI into irrigation systems: from planning to implementation**
   - Selection of technologies for implementation
   - Monitoring and automation systems
   - Practical implementation of precision irrigation technologies
5. **Technologies and innovations in precision irrigation**
   - Drip irrigation and underground systems
   - Using drones and satellite data to optimize irrigation
   - Software for managing irrigation systems
6. **Economic efficiency of implementation of AI technologies**
   - Cost estimation for the implementation of innovations
   - How automation reduces water costs

- Return on investment in AI-based irrigation systems

7. **Management of water resources in the conditions of climate change**
    - Impact of climate change on water resources
    - Strategies for adaptation of agriculture to new realities
    - Precision irrigation as a means of combating climate challenges

8. **Legal and environmental aspects of AI implementation**
    - Legal requirements for the use of AI
    - Environmental benefits of precision irrigation
    - State support and regulation of water resources

9. **Practical cases of AI application in different cultures**
    - Grain irrigation, viticulture, horticulture and vegetable crops
    - Successful examples of AI implementation on farms

10. **Conclusions and prospects for development**
    - The benefits of artificial intelligence for precision irrigation
    - Future trends in the development of irrigation technologies
    - Recommendations for farmers on the implementation of innovations

Appendices

- Overview of technology tools and software for precision irrigation
- Useful resources and literature for further study

Introduction:

Why precision irrigation is the future of agriculture

In today's world, where climate change and scarcity of resources have become global challenges, agriculture is also forced to adapt to new realities. Traditional methods of farming are no longer able to meet the needs of humanity. The issue of water resources is becoming increasingly acute, and farmers around the world are looking for innovative ways to optimize their use. One such method is precision irrigation using artificial intelligence (AI).

Why is water a strategic resource?

Water is the most precious resource needed for life on Earth, and it is crucial for agriculture. However, many countries are already facing its shortage. World statistics show that more than 70% of fresh water is spent on field irrigation. These are huge volumes, and if left unchecked, the consequences can be catastrophic for both farmers and the planet.

Advice: "Conserve water as carefully as you conserve crops. The rational use of water resources is not only a saving of money, but also an investment in the future."

Precision irrigation: What is it and how does it work?

Precision irrigation is an innovative technology that allows you to supply water only when and where it is needed. Using sensor systems, moisture sensors, weather data and artificial intelligence algorithms, farmers can achieve optimal water distribution for each plant. This is not just "smart" irrigation - it is a new approach to growing plants that takes into account the specific needs of each crop in different phases of its growth.

Quote: "Saving every drop of water today means securing a crop tomorrow," John Smith, a California farmer who switched to artificial irrigation.

Problems of traditional irrigation methods

Traditional irrigation, which has been used by farmers for centuries, has a number of disadvantages. Water is supplied unevenly, a large part of it evaporates or is absorbed by the soil, which leads to excessive costs and depletion of water resources. This not only affects the economics of farming, but also poses threats to the environment.

Disadvantages of traditional irrigation:

- **High water losses.** Water evaporates or flows to places where it is not needed.
- **Uneconomical.** Due to the unevenness of irrigation, significant resources are wasted.
- **Impact on the harvest.** Too much or too little water can negatively affect plant growth.

Advice: "If you're still using traditional irrigation, consider switching over to a gradually more accurate system that will allow you to conserve water and improve yields."

Innovations in the agricultural sector: Artificial intelligence for irrigation

Artificial intelligence has not only changed many aspects of our lives, but is also being actively implemented in agriculture. Modern irrigation systems that use AI are able to analyze data from sensors, predict the weather and make decisions about when and how much water to apply to the field. This allows you to avoid overspending of resources and significantly increases the efficiency of farming.

Example: An Arizona farmer who used an AI irrigation system was able to reduce water costs by 40% in one year while increasing yields by 15%.

Cons of using AI in irrigation:

- **Initial costs.** Implementing technology can be expensive.
- **The need for training.** Staff training is required to use such systems.
- **Technical support.** Systems may require maintenance and ongoing monitoring.

Technologies that are changing agriculture

Today, precision irrigation is becoming more accessible thanks to the introduction of new technologies. Using drones to monitor plant health, weather stations to collect weather data, and sensors to measure soil moisture allows farmers to quickly adapt to changes in the environment and make informed decisions.

Advice: "Invest in modern monitoring technologies. They will help you quickly respond to climate change and optimize processes in the field."

Is your farm ready for precision irrigation?

The introduction of new technologies requires readiness for change. Before starting to use precision irrigation, a farmer should assess his resources and capabilities. Although the system may seem expensive in the initial stages, its cost-effectiveness pays off in the long run.

Advantages of implementing precise irrigation:

- **Saving resources.** Water costs are significantly reduced.
- **Increase in productivity.** Plants get optimal conditions for growth.
- **Reducing the impact on the environment.** Rational use of water resources reduces the ecological footprint.

Precision irrigation is not only a modern technology, but also a necessity for farmers who want to use resources efficiently and preserve the environment. Thanks to artificial intelligence, this process becomes even more accurate and efficient. In the following chapters of the book, we will consider in more detail how to implement these technologies in practice and how they can bring real benefits to your farm.

Quote at the end of the introduction: "The future of agriculture is smart solutions that help save resources and increase yields," says Dr. Agnes Miller, agrotechnology expert.

Chapter 1:

Basics of Precision Irrigation

Irrigation is one of the most important elements of agricultural production. It provides plants with water, without which their growth is impossible. But traditional irrigation methods are not always effective. They can lead to excessive water consumption, which is especially critical in the face of climate change. That is why precision irrigation has become an important tool for modern farmers.

What is precision irrigation and its advantages?

Precision irrigation is a technology that allows you to control the supply of water to plants with maximum precision. The main goal is to provide exactly the amount of water that the culture needs at a specific moment. This allows not only to save water resources, but also to improve the quality of the crop.

Advice: "For a better distribution of water, it is worth considering not only the type of soil, but also the microclimate of your region. Using soil moisture sensors will help to adjust the irrigation system more precisely."

Traditional irrigation methods and their limitations

Traditional irrigation, such as surface or sprinkler irrigation, has a number of disadvantages. The main thing is uneven soil moisture. This leads to the fact that part of the plants receives too much water, and the other part suffers from its lack. In addition, a significant amount of water evaporates before it reaches the root system.

Disadvantages of traditional irrigation:

- **Uneconomical.** A large amount of water is lost through evaporation.
- **Uneven hydration** Plants can receive uneven amount of water
- **Maintenance costs.** Traditional systems require more manual work and maintenance.

Quote: "Irrigation is a balance between the amount of water and the needs of the plants. The use of AI allows this balance to be achieved with maximum precision" — agricultural technology expert Michael Williams.

How is AI changing approaches to irrigation?

Artificial intelligence (AI) allows you to completely rethink the irrigation process. It uses data from sensors and monitoring systems to automatically control the water supply. AI analyzes soil moisture, weather conditions and even weather forecasts to make real-time decisions. This allows not only to save water, but also to increase productivity.

Advantages of using AI:

- **Saving water.** AI determines exactly how much water each plant needs.
- **Process automation.** The system works autonomously, with minimal human intervention.
- **Increase in productivity.** Optimal irrigation ensures better plant growth.

Cons:

- **Cost of implementation.** The technology can be expensive in the initial stages.
- **The need for maintenance.** AI systems require regular monitoring and tuning.

Advice: "If you want to implement AI for precision irrigation, start by testing on a small area of your farm. This will help you evaluate the effectiveness without a large investment."

Water resources monitoring and management technologies

Modern irrigation systems use a variety of monitoring technologies. Soil moisture sensors measure how much water is already in the soil, and weather stations provide accurate data on weather conditions. AI processes this data and determines when and how much water should be given.

Example: Farmer Johnson from California used an AI system to irrigate his vineyard. With the help of sensors and weather forecasts, the system automatically regulated water supply This allowed him to reduce water consumption by 35% and at the same time get 20% more harvest.

Advice: "Don't forget to check the system settings regularly. Seasonal changes can affect the irrigation efficiency, so it's better to adjust the parameters depending on the climatic conditions."

This approach to precision irrigation allows for significant resource savings, increased farm efficiency, and reduced environmental impact. By using AI, farmers can not only improve crop quality, but also reduce water and system maintenance costs.

Chapter 2:

The Role of Artificial Intelligence in Irrigation Monitoring and Management

Artificial intelligence (AI) is becoming increasingly important for managing processes in agriculture, particularly for irrigation systems. Thanks to accurate forecasts, automated processes and big data analysis, AI can help optimize water use and reduce costs while ensuring high yields. This section describes how AI is used in irrigation monitoring and management systems, which specific technologies are used, and how it affects farm economic performance.

Example 1: Using sensors and AI in an automated irrigation system

Machinery:
Many modern irrigation systems use soil moisture sensors installed directly in the field. These sensors measure the moisture level at different depths, which allows you to get accurate data about the condition of the soil under the plants. Usually, such sensors work on the basis of the capacitive or time-domain reflectometry (TDR) method of measuring humidity, which provide results in the form of digital data.

How AI is involved in this:
AI analyzes this data in real-time, comparing it to previous readings and weather forecasts. Based on the received information, the system decides when and how much water should be used to irrigate each section of the field. The system also takes into account factors such as soil type, amount of sunlight, and even wind direction.

Economic part:
According to research, automated irrigation systems using AI can reduce water consumption by an average of 25-30%. This is achieved by accurately determining the needs of plants, which reduces the risk of excessive watering. In addition, farmers save up to 20% on fertilizers, since optimal irrigation promotes uniform plant growth, which requires smaller doses of fertilizers.

Advice:
"Use moisture sensors in combination with AI predictions to avoid overwatering and save resources. Investment in sensors and NE can pay off in the first two or three seasons."

Example 2: Using drones to analyze the state of fields

Machinery:
Drones equipped with high resolution cameras and multispectral sensors, help farmers get detailed images of

fields. They are able to capture images in different light spectrums, such as infrared and ultraviolet radiation, which allows them to detect signs of plant stress, lack of moisture or nutrients.

How AI is involved in this:

AI analyzes the collected images to identify areas where additional irrigation or fertilizer application is needed. An important part of this process is recognizing patterns in images, which can indicate problems that the naked eye may not always see. Thanks to the analysis of satellite and drone data, AI can develop individual irrigation regimes for each zone of the field.

Economic part:

The use of drones in combination with AI makes it possible to reduce fuel and labor costs, as there is no need for frequent inspections of the fields. According to estimates, farmers can save up to 15-20% of working time. In addition, costs for fertilizers and other agrochemicals are reduced due to the fact that the irrigation system becomes more targeted and works only where it is necessary.

Quote:

"Using drones helps me monitor large areas of land without spending a lot of time. AI analyzes data faster and *more accurately than any agronomist." — Mark Brown, a farmer from Canada.*

Example 3: Intelligent weather stations and their impact on the irrigation process

Machinery:
Smart weather stations are installed in fields to collect information about weather conditions such as temperature, humidity, precipitation and wind speed. They work continuously, sending data to a central server for analysis.

How AI is involved in this:
AI uses this data to make predictions and plan irrigation processes. For example, if rainfall is forecast, the system can automatically delay watering to avoid excessive water use. In addition, based on temperature and humidity data, the AI adjusts the amount of water applied to each section of the field.

Economic part:
Weather stations with AI allow you to reduce irrigation costs by 15-25%, as the system takes into account the weather forecast and adjusts processes automatically. This not only saves water, but also reduces energy costs, since the pumps only work when it is really necessary.

Advice:

"Invest in intelligent weather stations if your fields are located in regions with unstable weather conditions. This will allow you to manage the irrigation process more precisely and save resources."

Variable irrigation: an individual approach to each site

Variable irrigation systems are the technology of the future, already today

implemented on many farms. It allows you to adjust the amount of water supplied to different parts of the field, depending on the actual needs of the plants.

Machinery:
Variable irrigation uses a network of soil moisture sensors and drones to constantly monitor the condition of the soil and plants. The system determines which areas need more water and which need less, and automatically changes the watering intensity for each zone.

How AI is involved in this:
Artificial intelligence analyzes large volumes of data collected from various sources and creates a field irrigation map. Each zone of the field can receive a different amount of water depending on its condition, weather and soil type. This allows you to minimize water losses and increase the efficiency of irrigation.

Economic part:
Variable irrigation systems make it possible to reduce water consumption by 30-40%. Additionally, it reduces energy costs because the pumps only work when needed and for the amount of water that is really needed. Farmers also save on fertilizer costs because even watering helps plants absorb nutrients better.

Quote:
"Variable irrigation in my fields has cut water costs almost in half. The AI clearly identifies the needs of each zone, and I no longer worry about overwatering or drought." — Anna Lind, a farmer from Sweden.

Advice:
"Consider rotating irrigation, especially if you have different soil types in the same field. This will make more efficient use of water resources and increase yields."

Artificial intelligence opens up vast opportunities for efficient irrigation management in agriculture. By utilizing advanced technologies, farmers can significantly reduce water, electricity, and fertilizer costs while increasing yields and optimizing production processes. Investments in AI and sensor systems can pay off in just a few seasons, with long-term benefits ensuring stable business growth.

Chapter 4:

Integrating AI into Irrigation Systems: From Planning to Implementation

A precision irrigation system is not just a set of technologies. It is an entire ecosystem in which artificial intelligence (AI) helps make decisions at every stage. In this section, we'll look at how to integrate AI into your irrigation system. What technologies will you need? How to plan implementation? And what economic benefits can you get?

1. Selection of technologies for integration

Before you begin, consider what technology you need. It is important to know that the right sensors and software can significantly increase the efficiency of irrigation.

Types of sensors:

1. **Humidity sensors**: They measure soil moisture in real time.
    - *Example*: System *Decagon Devices* can accurately measure humidity, which allows you to save water.

2. **Weather stations**: They record temperature fluctuations, rainfall and other meteorological indicators.
    - *Quote*: *"Without weather information, you are blind in your irrigation management"* — agronomy expert John Smith.
3. **Cameras for monitoring the condition of plants**: They help assess plant health by detecting problems in the early stages.
    - *Advice*: Choose cameras with image analysis functionality to automate the monitoring process.

2. Development of a management system

Once the technologies are selected, the next step is to design the control system. You have to figure out how the sensors and the software will work together.

Software for data analysis:

- **Platforms**: Use specialized platforms such as *FarmLogs* or *CropX*, for data collection and analysis.
- **Automation**: Integrate NE for automatic control of the irrigation system. This will allow you to react to changes in growing conditions instantly.

Example: A farmer in Texas uses a platform *Agrian*, which automatically adjusts irrigation depending on sensor data. This allows him to save up to 40% of water.

Technical aspects: It is important to set up the communication between the sensors and the software correctly. Use Wi-Fi or Bluetooth for convenience.

3. Implementation planning

After developing the system, you need to prepare an implementation plan. This can take time, but proper planning will help you avoid mistakes.

Steps for implementation:

1. **Assessment of resources**: Analyze what resources you need to implement.
    - *Advice*: Always have a contingency plan in case of unexpected expenses.
2. **System testing**: Test before implementation. This will help identify possible flaws.
    - *Example*: Farmers in California tested the new sensors on small plots, avoiding significant costs in case of failure.
3. **Implementation and training**: After testing, proceed to full implementation. Do not forget to train employees to use new technologies.

- *Quote*: "Technologies without knowledge are just expensive toys" — Jane Doe, agronomist.

4. Evaluation of economic efficiency: detailed metrics

Estimating the cost-effectiveness of a precision irrigation system is an important step in helping you understand how the technology affects your business. In this section, we will look at how to measure water costs, yields and total costs to get a clear picture of the effectiveness of technology implementation.

1. Measurement of water consumption

Saving water is one of the main advantages of precision irrigation systems. To accurately measure your water consumption, follow these steps:

Steps to measure:

1. Data collection: Install water meters on irrigation systems. They should be located at strategic points to ensure accurate measurements.
    - *Advice*: Use automated meters that can transmit data in real time.

2. **Consumption record**: Record the amount of water you use daily or weekly. Compare this data with previous seasons to identify changes.
    - *Example*: If you used 10,000 liters of water per hectare last year and 7,000 liters this year, you have saved 30%.
3. **Calculation of savings**: Use the formula:
Water savings=Expenditure in the past−Expenditure in the current year

2. Measurement of productivity

Yield is a key indicator of irrigation efficiency. To estimate the yield, you should:

Steps to measure:

1. **Harvest data collection**: Identify the area under cultivation and record the yield.
    - *Example*: If you grew 5 tons of wheat per hectare, record this value.
2. **Use of standard units**: Measure yields in standard units (eg tons per hectare). This will allow you to compare results with different crops or in different seasons.
3. **Comparison with previous results**: Compare new data with previous seasons to determine increases or decreases in yield.

- *Quote*: "Yields are a mirror of your agribusiness. Changes in irrigation are reflected in crop yields." — agronomist Oleksandr Ivanenko.
4. Calculation: Use the formula:
Yield=Harvest volume (tons) : Area (hectares)

3. Determination of total costs

Determining the total costs will help you understand how profitable the implemented system was. Include all costs associated with irrigation.

Steps to determine total costs:

1. Capital Costs: Record all the costs of installing an irrigation system, including equipment, sensors, pipes, and other components.
   - *Example*: If the total capital expenditure was $15,000, record this amount.
2. Operating Costs: Include system maintenance costs, electricity, and irrigation staff wages.
   - *Advice*: Keep track of your monthly expenses to understand your total operating expenses for the year.
3. Total Costs: Add capital and operating costs to get total costs:
Total Costs=Capital Costs+Operating Costs

4. Cost Analysis: Compare total costs with water savings and increased yields. This will help you understand how profitable the implementation of the system was.

Example: If the total cost of irrigation was $10,000, and the water savings and increased yield yielded an additional $12,000, you had a net profit of $2,000.

Technical details: Use farm management software (FMS) that automatically generates reports to collect and analyze data.

Integrating AI into irrigation systems is not just a technological innovation. This is an opportunity to significantly improve the efficiency of your agribusiness. From the right choice of technologies to competent planning and evaluation of economic benefits — every stage is important. Technologies open new horizons, but their effectiveness depends on your approach and readiness for change.

Chapter 5:

Technologies and Innovations in Precision Irrigation

In this section, we will look at the main technologies used in precision irrigation systems. This analysis will help you understand how technology affects the efficiency of agricultural production, increasing yields and reducing costs. Technologies are not just tools. They can be a game changer in your agribusiness.

1. Basic technologies of precise irrigation

1.1. Drip irrigation

Drip irrigation is a method in which water is supplied directly to the roots of plants through drippers. This method is very effective because it minimizes water consumption and reduces the risk of disease development.

Pros:

- **Water saving:** Only the necessary amount of water is used.
- **Improvement of crop quality:** The ability to control the supply of water and fertilizers.

- **Cost reduction:** Less water means less costs.

Cons:

- **Installation costs:** Upfront costs can be high.
- **Need for service:** Systems can become clogged, requiring regular maintenance.

1.2. Underground irrigation

This method involves installing pipes underground to deliver water directly to plant roots. It can be especially useful in areas with limited access to water.

Pros:

- **Reduction of evaporation:** The water does not evaporate because it is supplied underground.
- **Savings on maintenance:** Reduces the need for frequent watering.

Cons:

- **Difficulty of installation:** It is necessary to carry out ground work.
- **Difficulty of repair:** Repair costs can be high.

Tip: Before installing subsurface irrigation, consult with a professional to assess your field's needs.

1.3. Automated irrigation systems

These systems use sensors to monitor soil moisture, temperature and other parameters, automatically adjusting the water supply.

Pros:

- **Convenience:** Automatic irrigation control reduces the need for manual intervention.
- **Optimization of resources:** Water savings thanks to precise regulation.

Cons:

- **Equipment costs:** Upfront costs for sensors and software can be high.
- **Dependence on technologies:** If the system crashes, it can lead to problems.

2. Use of sensor technologies

2.1. Humidity sensors

These sensors measure soil moisture in real time. They help determine when and how much water should be given.

Tip: Install sensors at different depths to get a complete moisture picture.

Example: One farmer installed sensors at a depth of 30 cm and 60 cm, which allowed him to reduce irrigation costs by 25% per season.

2.2. Temperature sensors

Soil temperature affects plant growth. The use of sensors helps to adapt irrigation to changes in temperature.

Pros:

- **Change control:** Allows you to quickly react to changes in the weather.
- **Improving yield:** Studies have shown that the correct temperature increases the yield by 15%.

Cons:

- **Service costs:** Sensors may require calibration.

3. Irrigation management software

Management programs allow farmers to receive analytics that help in decision-making. They can be connected to sensors and automate the system.

Pros:

- **Data analysis:** Easy to get performance reports.
- **Accessibility:** Many programs have mobile versions for easy access.

Cons:

- **Difficulty of use:** It is necessary to spend time on learning.
- **Subscription costs:** Some programs have a monthly fee.

Tip: Choose an app that offers a free version to test its functionality.

4. Economic benefit from precision irrigation technologies

The implementation of precision irrigation technologies has numerous economic benefits. Reduced water costs, increased productivity and reduced labor costs are just a few.

4.1. Examples of benefits

Example: A tomato farmer has implemented drip irrigation. His water bill used to be $2,000 a year. After implementing the system, they dropped to $1,200. And the yield increased by 30%.

4.2. Return on investment

To determine your return on investment (ROI), you should calculate:

$$ROI = \text{Money saved} - \text{Installation costs} / \text{Installation costs} \times 100\%$$

This will help to understand when the investment will start to bring profit.

Precision irrigation technologies are your key to success in agriculture. They will not only help save resources, but also provide you with a stable income. Do not be afraid to implement new solutions, because it is innovation that leads to success. If you have additional questions or need examples, please let me know!

Chapter 6:

Economic efficiency and profitability of AI implementation

In modern agribusiness, it is important not only to implement new technologies, but also to evaluate their economic efficiency. In this section, we look at the costs of implementing artificial intelligence (AI) technologies for irrigation, how automation reduces water costs, the economic benefits of reducing water loss, and the return on investment in AI for farms of various sizes.

6.1. Costs of implementing AI technologies for irrigation

Implementing AI for irrigation requires upfront costs. This includes:

- **Purchase of equipment:** These can be humidity sensors, automated control systems and drones.
- **Software:** It is necessary to provide access to analytical platforms that process data.
- **Staff training:** It is necessary to teach employees to work with new technologies.

Cost advantages:

- **Reducing costs in the future:** Although the initial costs may be high, this results in significant savings over time.
- **Productivity improvement:** Irrigation automation allows farmers to work more efficiently.

Disadvantages of costs:

- **High initial investment:** Many farmers may not be able to immediately invest in new technologies.
- **Risk of unforeseen costs:** For example, if there are technical problems.

"Investing in AI for irrigation isn't just a cost, it's your path to the future."

6.2. How automation cuts water costs

Automated irrigation systems allow you to save water. AI analyzes data on soil moisture and weather conditions, optimizing the time and amount of watering.

Tip: Use moisture sensors to determine exactly when to water your plants.

Example: Farmer Olena implemented an automated irrigation system. It reduced water consumption by 30% thanks to precise control of irrigation.

Pros:

- **Reducing water costs:** Automation allows you to avoid overspending.
- **Improving plant health:** Proper watering promotes better development of the root system.

Cons:

- **Need for maintenance:** Systems require regular maintenance.
- **Possible malfunctions:** In the event of a system malfunction, there may be a lack of water.

"A system that saves water is not just a benefit, it's our responsibility."

6.3. Assessment of economic benefits from reducing water losses

Reducing water costs has a direct impact on farm income. When water is used more efficiently, farmers can reduce irrigation costs.

Tip: Conduct regular assessments of water costs and their impact on profits.

Example: A farmer implemented a new technology that reduced irrigation costs by 20%. This allowed him to increase profits by 15% during the year.

Pros:

- **Increase in profitability:** A reduction in irrigation costs directly affects profits.
- **Stimulation of development:** More money to invest in other technologies.

Cons:

- **Unforeseen changes:** Water costs may vary depending on the season.
- **Technical problems:** System failures are possible, which can lead to increased costs.

"Every drop of water is money. By reducing losses, we ensure the future.".

6.4. Return on investment in AI for farms of different scales

The return on investment (ROI) in AI technologies is determined primarily by the economic benefits they bring.

Tip: Conduct ROI analysis after implementing new technologies.

Example: A small vegetable farm invested in AI to automate irrigation. During the first year, the profitability was 120%, thanks to the reduction of water costs and the increase in yield.

Pros:

- **High profitability:** Many farms note the positive impact of AI implementation on income.
- **Flexibility:** AI technologies can be adapted to the needs of farms of various scales.

Cons:

- **Long payback period:** Some farmers may need more time to experience the benefits.
- **Dependence on technologies:** The risk of problems in the event of a system failure increases.

The implementation of AI in agribusiness is a powerful tool for increasing economic efficiency and profitability. Although the initial costs may be high, the benefits of reduced water costs and increased yields far outweigh these costs. In today's world, it is important not only to implement new technologies, but also to evaluate their impact on business. Therefore, investing in AI can become a key stage in the development of farming, which strives for success and sustainable growth.

Chapter 7:

Water Resources Management in Climate Change

Water management is becoming an increasingly complex task in a world where the climate is constantly changing. This chapter focuses on how climate change affects water resources, strategic solutions for water management using AI, forecasting water needs in different climates, and the role of precision irrigation in climate change adaptation.

7.1. How climate change affects water resources

Climate change has a direct impact on the availability and quality of water resources. Rising temperatures, changes in precipitation and the frequency of extreme weather events affect water supplies.

Problems that arise:

- **Reduction of water reserves:** In many regions, there is a decrease in the water level in rivers and reservoirs.
- **Deterioration of water quality:** High temperatures can lead to algal blooms and pollution.

"Climate change is not just an environmental issue. It's also an economic security issue."

Example: In the southern regions of Ukraine, due to climate change, the water level in rivers decreased by 30%, which significantly affected agriculture.

Tip: Regularly analyze data on water resources in your area to understand trends and change your management strategy.

7.2. Strategic solutions for water management with the help of AI

Artificial intelligence offers new opportunities for effective management of water resources. It allows accurate monitoring and forecasting, which greatly facilitates the management process.

Examples of strategies:

- **Real-time monitoring:** Systems with sensors can provide data on water level, temperature and humidity.
- **Forecasting needs:** AI can analyze weather data and plant needs to optimize water use.

Pros:

- **Increasing efficiency:** Automation of water management helps to reduce costs.
- **Loss reduction:** Accurate data allows you to avoid overspending of water.

Cons:

- **High initial costs:** Implementation of systems may require significant financial investments.
- **Technical failures:** Dependence on technology can lead to problems if it malfunctions.

"Water is life. Water management should be science, not luck."

7.3. Prediction of water needs in different climatic conditions

Forecasting water needs in different climatic conditions is critical for effective resource management. Changes in climate can significantly affect the water needs of plants.

Tip: Use models to predict water needs depending on different weather conditions.

Example: The farmer, thanks to the analysis of climate data, changed the irrigation schedule. This allowed him to reduce irrigation costs by 25%.

Pros:

- **Cost optimization:** Accurate forecasting allows you to avoid overspending of water.
- **Increase in yield:** Providing plants with the necessary amount of water improves their development.

Cons:

- **Unforeseen changes:** Weather can be unpredictable and forecasts are not always accurate.
- **Research costs:** Development of forecasting models may require additional costs.

"Prediction is our future. You can't trust chance when it comes to water."

7.4. The role of precision irrigation in adaptation to climate change

Precision irrigation is an important tool for adapting agriculture to climate change. It allows you to reduce water consumption and increase the efficiency of irrigation.

Tip: Invest in precision irrigation technology to reap the full benefits.

Pros:

- **Water saving:** Precision irrigation makes it possible to use water more efficiently.
- **Soil conservation:** Less water reduces the risk of erosion and improves soil health.

Cons:

- **High equipment costs:** The initial investment in precision irrigation systems can be large.
- **Technical problems:** Need regular maintenance.

"Precision irrigation is key to surviving climate change."

Water resource management in the face of climate change requires new approaches and technologies. The use of AI, precision irrigation and forecasting of water needs helps to adapt to changes and conserve water resources. It is important to consider both the pros and cons of introducing new technologies. Only in this way will agricultural producers be able to effectively manage water and ensure a stable harvest in changing conditions.

Chapter 8:

Legal and Environmental Aspects of Using AI for Irrigation

The use of artificial intelligence (AI) in agriculture, in particular in irrigation systems, is becoming an important tool for improving the efficiency of water resources use. However, it also involves a number of legal and environmental aspects. In this section, we will consider legal requirements, environmental benefits, regulation of water resources, and the role of government support in the implementation of new technologies.

8.1. Legal requirements for the use of AI systems in agriculture

Before implementing AI systems for irrigation, farmers must consider legal requirements. This includes legislation governing water use as well as requirements for the data collected by the systems.

Examples of legal requirements:

- **Licensing:** In some regions, the use of irrigation systems may require special licensing.

- **Data protection:** It is important to comply with regulations regarding the collection and processing of personal data if AI systems use user data.

Advice: Always consult an attorney to ensure compliance with all legal regulations.

8.2. Environmental benefits of precision irrigation with AI

The use of AI-assisted precision irrigation has numerous environmental benefits. This allows you to reduce water consumption, improve the quality of the soil and reduce the negative impact on the environment.

Main environmental benefits:

- **Reducing water consumption:** Precise irrigation helps to avoid excessive water consumption, which is critical in the face of climate change.
- **Conservation of natural resources:** Using less water helps preserve water resources for future generations.

Pros:

- **Environmental sustainability:** Reducing the impact on ecosystems.

- **Improving biodiversity:** Water conservation contributes to the preservation of natural biotopes.

Cons:

- **The need for technologies:** Effective implementation requires modern technologies, which can be costly.
- **Dependence on technologies:** Failures in systems can lead to negative consequences.

8.3. Regulation of the use of water resources and innovative technologies

Water regulation is an important aspect that affects the use of AI in irrigation. Laws and regulations determine how and when water resources can be used.

The main elements of regulation:

- **Limits on water use:** In many regions there are limits on the amount of water that farmers can use.
- **Reporting requirements:** Farmers may be required to report their water and irrigation use.

Advice: Research local laws and follow all regulations to avoid legal trouble.

8.4. The role of state support and grants in technology implementation

Government support plays a key role in the implementation of irrigation technologies. Grants and support programs can significantly reduce the costs of implementing AI systems.

Main forms of support:

- **Grants for the introduction of new technologies:** Many countries offer financing for farmers who implement green technologies.
- **Educational programs:** Government bodies can offer courses and training for farmers on the use of new technologies..

Pros:

- **Cost reduction:** Government support helps reduce the financial burden on farmers.
- **Awareness raising:** Educational programs contribute to the dissemination of knowledge about new technologies.

Cons:

- **Competition for grants:** Not all farmers can receive support due to limited resources.

- **Administrative difficulties:** Obtaining grants can be red tape.

The legal and environmental aspects of using AI for irrigation are important for agribusiness sustainability. Complying with legal requirements, understanding environmental benefits, regulating water use, and obtaining government support are key elements that will help farmers implement new technologies successfully. AI technologies can significantly improve water management, but it is important to consider all aspects of their use.

Chapter 9:

Case studies: implementing AI in different cultures

In this section, we will look at how artificial intelligence (AI) is changing irrigation approaches in different crops. In particular, we will focus on irrigation of grain crops, viticulture, horticulture and vegetable production. Examples of successful implementation of AI in real farms will show how new technologies can significantly increase efficiency and productivity.

9.1. Irrigation of grain crops with the help of AI

Example 1: "Green Lan" farm (Ukraine)

Technologies and methods:

- **Irrigation management platforms**: Usage **CropX**, which analyzes data from sensors to determine optimal irrigation.
- **Software**: **AgriWebb** — a farm management solution that integrates data on soil conditions and meteorology.

The results:

- **Reduction of water costs by 20%.**
- **15% yield increase.**

Advice: Update your software regularly to access new features.

9.2. Viticulture and horticulture: specifics of irrigation

Example 2: "Sunny" vineyard (Moldova)

Technologies and methods:

- **Platforms for monitoring: SmartIrrigation** — a system that allows you to control irrigation based on sensor data.
- **Software: Viticulturist** — a solution specially developed for vineyard management, which includes the functions of climate monitoring and yield analysis.

The results:

- **Cost optimization**: Irrigation costs decreased by 25%.
- **Improvement of crop quality.**

Advice: Invest in additional sensors for more accurate monitoring.

9.3. Precise irrigation for vegetable crops

Example 3: "Vegetable Valley" farm (Poland)

Technologies and methods:

- **Integrated solutions**: **Netafim** — a drip irrigation system with the possibility of integration with software for monitoring the condition of plants.
- **Software**: **Waterbit** — an irrigation automation platform that uses data on humidity and meteorological conditions.

The results:

- **Reduction of water costs by 40%.**
- **Increasing yield.**

Advice: Perform regular system checks to prevent leaks.

9.4. Examples of successful implementation on real farms

Example 4: "Fertile Land" farm (Ukraine)

Technologies and methods:

- **Management platforms**: **FarmLogs** — a system for monitoring and managing yield and irrigation data.
- **Software**: **Soil Moisture Sensor** — sensors for determining soil moisture, integrated with management platforms.

The results:

- **Save water by 30%.**
- **Up to 20% yield improvement.**

Advice: Use data from previous seasons to predict irrigation needs.

Example 5: Golden Vine Winery (Georgia)

Technologies and Methods:

- **Platforms for Monitoring:** *Wine Management System* — a solution designed to control the microclimate of vineyards.
- **Software:** *Agrivi* — a system for agribusiness management that includes yield data analysis.

Results:

- Improved grape quality.
- Increased demand for products.

Advice: Use Geographic Information Systems (GIS) to visualize data effectively.

Example 6: "Smachna Hryadka" Garden (Germany)

Technologies and methods:

- **Management systems: Dronedeploy** — a platform for drones that analyzes the condition of plants and optimizes irrigation.
- **Software: Irrigation Scheduler** — a program for planning and monitoring the irrigation system.

The results:

- **Reduction of water costs by 40%.**
- **High quality vegetables.**

Advice: Collaborate with technology companies to implement new solutions.

The benefits of AI for precision irrigation

The implementation of artificial intelligence in irrigation systems opens up new horizons for agribusiness. Here are some of the main benefits:

Saving resources. Thanks to accurate analysis of data on soil moisture and climatic conditions, farmers can reduce water consumption by up to 50%. *"I never thought I could* *save so much water,"* — shares the experience of one of the farmers who implemented an irrigation system based on AI.

Improvement of yield. Using data to optimize irrigation results in higher yields. For example, a farm in Moldova that implemented smart technologies increased the yield of grapes by 20%. This highlights the importance of precise irrigation to achieve quality results.

Cost reduction. AI helps reduce the overall maintenance costs of irrigation systems. Electricity costs are reduced thanks to the optimization of pump operation.

Environmental sustainability. By reducing water consumption, agricultural producers help preserve the ecosystem. It also affects the long-term sustainability of agriculture.

The future of precision irrigation in agriculture

The future of precision irrigation looks promising. Here are some major trends:

Integration of technologies. Irrigation systems will become even more integrated with IoT (Internet of Things) technologies. This will allow farmers to receive real-time data and manage irrigation systems remotely.

Development of algorithms. As the volume of data grows, AI algorithms will become more accurate in predicting plant needs. This means that farmers will be able to adapt their irrigation strategies according to changes in climate and other factors.

Flexibility of systems. Modernized irrigation systems will be flexible, allowing them to be adapted to different cultures and conditions. This will be an important factor for small and medium farmers.

Reducing the impact of climate change. In the conditions of global climate changes, precise irrigation technologies will help agricultural producers to adapt to new realities.

Recommendations for Farmers Who Want to Implement Innovative Irrigation Methods

For farmers looking to adapt their irrigation practices, here are some practical tips:

1. **Assessment of Needs**
   Start by analyzing your irrigation requirements. As one expert notes, *"Not all technologies are suitable for every crop."* Identify the specific needs of your fields and crops before making decisions.
2. **System Selection**
   Choose a system that aligns best with your

conditions. Consider platforms such as **CropX** or **Netafim**, which help automate irrigation processes efficiently.

3. **Investment in Technology**
   Invest in sensors and software to receive real-time data. This data enables informed decision-making and enhances precision.

4. **Employee Training**
   Provide training for your employees so they can effectively use the new systems. Well-trained staff can maximize the benefits of advanced technologies.

5. **Data Analysis**
   Regularly analyze the collected data to optimize your irrigation processes. Data collection is just the beginning—success lies in its proper interpretation and application.

6. **Collaboration with Experts**
   Work with agronomy and technology experts to ensure smooth implementation. Their expertise can help you avoid pitfalls and achieve better results.

7. **Experimentation**
   Be open to experimenting with new irrigation methods. As one farmer shares, *"We tried different approaches and eventually found the optimal one."*

8.

The Benefits of Artificial Intelligence in Irrigation

Introducing artificial intelligence into precision irrigation systems is a critical step for the future of agribusiness. AI-driven solutions help conserve resources, reduce waste, and improve crop quality. Farmers who embrace these innovations will gain a competitive edge, ensuring long-term sustainability and profitability.

Don't delay in adopting new technologies—they might be the key to success in your agribusiness.

Afterword

As we close the pages of this book, it's worth reflecting on the profound implications of integrating artificial intelligence into precision irrigation. The journey of agriculture, from traditional practices to the cutting-edge methods discussed here, represents more than just technological progress. It encapsulates a shift in how we interact with our environment, adapt to challenges, and prepare for the future.

The Intersection of Tradition and Innovation

Farming has always been a balancing act between nature's unpredictable rhythms and human ingenuity. Precision irrigation, powered by AI, takes this relationship to a new level. It combines the wisdom of generations with tools capable of making split-second decisions based on real-time data. Yet, this evolution does not erase the importance of intuition and experience. Instead, it enhances them.

For example, a farmer in California struggling with drought can use AI-driven systems to manage scarce water resources effectively, while still relying on their understanding of the land to decide which crops to prioritize. This partnership between technology and human insight is the cornerstone of sustainable agriculture.

A Look at the Bigger Picture

At its heart, precision irrigation isn't just about improving yields or cutting costs—it's about sustainability. Water is life, not just for crops but for entire ecosystems. AI technologies allow us to respect this resource by using it wisely. By monitoring soil moisture, predicting weather patterns, and automating irrigation schedules, we minimize waste and protect the planet.

From a sociological perspective, this shift has ripple effects. Regions that adopt precision irrigation can experience enhanced food security, economic stability, and community resilience. Small-scale farmers, often the backbone of rural economies, can compete more effectively when equipped with affordable AI tools. This democratization of technology bridges the gap between industrial-scale operations and individual growers.

The Ethical Landscape

No innovation comes without ethical considerations. The integration of AI into agriculture raises questions about data ownership, equitable access, and environmental responsibility. Who owns the data collected by sensors?

How can smallholders in developing countries gain access to these technologies without being priced out?

These questions demand proactive policies and transparent discussions. Governments, tech developers, and farmers must collaborate to create frameworks that ensure fairness and inclusivity. AI's potential is vast, but it must be guided by a shared vision that prioritizes people and the planet over profits.

Overcoming Challenges

Every farmer knows that no growing season is without its challenges. The same applies to adopting precision irrigation systems. High initial costs, technical learning curves, and the need for infrastructure updates can deter adoption. However, as we've seen in successful case studies, these barriers can be overcome.

Take the example of a vineyard in France, where the integration of AI technology resulted in a 20% reduction in water use without sacrificing grape quality. The key? Strategic investments, robust training programs, and partnerships with agronomy experts.

A Vision for the Future

The future of precision irrigation is one of constant evolution. Emerging technologies like edge computing, blockchain for data security, and advanced machine learning algorithms promise even greater efficiency and accessibility. Imagine a world where farmers can control their entire irrigation system from a smartphone app, receive alerts about potential pest infestations, and adjust watering schedules based on hyper-local climate forecasts—all in real-time.

Yet, as technology advances, we must remain grounded in the principles of sustainability and community. The goal isn't just to grow more crops but to grow them better: in harmony with nature, with minimal environmental impact, and with maximum social benefit.

Practical Takeaways for Farmers

For farmers ready to take the leap into precision irrigation, the path begins with small steps:

- **Start Small**: Test AI-driven systems on a small plot before scaling up.
- **Seek Support**: Partner with local agricultural cooperatives or tech providers for training and resources.
- **Focus on ROI**: Prioritize systems with clear benefits, such as water-saving technologies or yield-boosting software.

- **Stay Informed**: Agriculture is ever-changing. Stay updated on new tools, techniques, and regulations.

A Call to Action

The integration of AI in precision irrigation is not just an opportunity but a responsibility. Each drop of water saved, each plant nourished more efficiently, and each farmer empowered by technology contributes to a global effort to secure our food systems against the challenges of tomorrow.

Let this book serve not just as a guide but as an invitation. An invitation to innovate, collaborate, and cultivate not just crops but a future where technology and tradition grow side by side. Together, we can transform agriculture into a beacon of sustainability, resilience, and prosperity.

Maxwell Steinbeck

Appendices

Overview of technological tools for precision irrigation

Precision irrigation systems are becoming increasingly popular among agricultural producers. Here is an overview of some of the main technological tools that can help optimize the irrigation process:

1. **Soil moisture sensors**
    - **Look**: Sensors can be divided into different types such as capacitive, resistive and strain gauges.
    - **Functions**: Measure the level of moisture in the soil, which allows you to determine exactly when you need to water.
2. **Irrigation management systems**
    - **Examples: Rain Bird, Hunter**.
    - **Functions**: Automate the irrigation process based on data received from sensors.
3. **Drones and satellite technologies**
    - **Examples: DJI Phantom, Center**.
    - **Functions**: Used to monitor the condition of the fields, identify areas with insufficient moisture.
4. **Platforms for data analysis**

- **Examples**: **CropX**, **AgriWebb**.
   - **Functions**: Collects and analyzes data from multiple sources, allowing the farmer to make informed irrigation decisions.
5. **Automated irrigation systems**
   - **Examples**: **Netafim**, **Valley Irrigation**.
   - **Functions**: Use technologies to automatically adjust watering modes based on weather conditions and plant needs.

List of available programs for monitoring water resources

Here are some programs that can help with water monitoring:

1. **WaterMinder**
   - **Functions**: Helps monitor water consumption and optimize its use.
2. **HydroLynx**
   - **Functions**: Provides water level data and real-time monitoring capability.
3. **AquaCrop**
   - **Functions**: A tool for modeling and managing water resources in fields.
4. **ET-Calculator**

- **Functions**: Calculates evaporation and irrigation needs based on climate conditions.
5. **Smart Irrigation**
    - **Functions**: Provides watering recommendations based on weather and soil moisture data.

Links to resources for more information

1. **International Irrigation and Drainage Association (ICID)**
    - ICID — a resource for obtaining information about irrigation practices and technologies.
2. **FAO (Food and Agriculture Organization of the United Nations)**
    - FAO Water — publications and research on water resources in agriculture.
3. **AgFunder Network Partners**
    - AgFunder — a platform for investments in agricultural technologies, with useful articles and news.
4. **The Climate Corporation**
    - Climate — programs for monitoring and managing agriculture using weather data.
5. **Precision Agriculture Association**
    - ON — a resource containing useful articles and research on precision agriculture.

www.ingramcontent.com/pod-product-compliance
Lightning Source LLC
Chambersburg PA
CBHW030049230526
45471CB00003B/1006